CHILD ABUSES AND THEIR RIGHTS IN INDIA

VOLUME 2, ISSUE 1 OF BRAIN BOOSTER ARTICLES

ARNAV KUMAR

Contents

Preface

"Start writing, no matter what. The water does not flow until the faucet is turned on".

-Louis L'Amour

Hundreds of students and professors are contributing their work to Brain Booster Articles, we are here to provide ample information about Law and Contemporary issues. Our aim is to provide a platform for today's generation to express their views and ideas on law and contemporary law.

Publication

This research paper is published in volume 2, issue 1 of Brain Booster Articles

Author

Arnav Kumar

CHAPTER ONE

Abstract

"Stop trying to turn children into someone they are not. Instead, let them unfold into who no human can imagine them to be."

-Vince Gowmon

The aim of this paper is to highlight the rights of children and the various types of child abuse, which are committed in India. The aim of the paper is to give a solution to how child abuse can cope up. The paper wants to convey that even though children have numerous rights but still they are not working properly. So to how the rights that are given by the Constitution of India can be protected and how we can cope up with child abuse, which is committed on the daily basis is to be discussed in this paper. The aim of the paper is to form people who realize the pain child suffers in silence. The aim of this paper is to give critical insights on the abuses of children that are being committed on daily basis. The aim of this paper is to offer a new perspective by which a child can be protected from their abuses.

CHAPTER TWO

Introduction

Providing education is the most effective effort for controlling child abuses.Child abuse is a violation of a fundamental human right that goes mostly unrecognised and unacknowledged. Child abuse and its negligence is a societal and public health issue, which can lead to long lasting effects into adulthood. However, all children that are exposed to abuse and mistreatment, are not affected the same. For some, the consequences of abuse could belong and devastating; others could experience less severe results. A child refers to anyone who is below the age of 18 (legally the age is different in different countries).[1] Legally they are unable to make their own decisions and hence they are under the care of parents or other caretaker. As we moved to development we moved to crimes. The crime towards children is on high. Violence against child is a taboo to the society. It is done physically, emotionally as well as sexually. Sometimes it involves neglect as well. This is practiced at home, school, institution, workplaces, in travel and tourism facilities, within communities. Etc. It causes harm and pain to a child which can even leads to death. It causes endless harm to dignity of that child which is an obstacle in their future development. Child abuse is a significant but preventable adverse childhood experience. Violence against children may be a gross violation of children's rights. Yet it's a worldwide reality across all countries and social groups. Increasingly, the Internet and mobile phones also put children at risk of abuse as some adults look to the Internet to pursue sexual relationships with children.The volume and circulation of photographs of child abuse is also on the rise. Children themselves also send each other sexualized messages or images on their mobile phones, so called 'sexting',[2] which puts them in peril for other abuse. When children get separated from their families, left without protection, they're easy prey for traffickers to take advantage of either by force or with false promises. This is one of the most dangerous things going on these days.

[1] The Majority Act, 1875 India, available at: http://legislative.gov.in/actsofparliamentfromtheyear (last visited on October 19, 2020).

[2]Sexting by children, available at: https://www.theguardian.com/society/2019/dec/30/ (last visited on October 19, 2020).

CHAPTER THREE

Types of violence

I. **Physical/ Maltreatment** – It includes violent punishment, Intimate partner violence etc. Intimate partner violence (controlling behaviours by a partner) increases the risks ofemotional and physiological problems and change in behaviour of a child. Sometimes they are beaten while having sex or for no reason.

II. **Sexual** – They are forced for sex (different positions) or raped. Sometimes they are manipulated for prostitution or forced to get into it and provide sex to customers. Perpetrators can be family members or strangers or seniors, etc.

III. **Psychological / Emotional** - They can get mentally so down which can leads to anxiety, depression and many kind of mental health issues such as anger, stress, inter personal problems, self mutilation, unsafe or dysfunctional sexual behaviour.

IV. **Child exploitation** - Commercial sexual exploitation of youngsters may be a commercial transaction that involves the sexual exploitation of a toddler, like the prostitution of youngsters, kiddie porn, child labour, slavery, trafficking of children and child sexual molestation.Child exploitation is defined as the use of children for the benefit or profit of others, resulting in the child's unjust, cruel, and hurtful treatment. These activities are obstacle to the child's physical or mental health, education, moral or social-emotional development. Child work refers to the participation of youngsters in an economic activity. Child labour refers to all kinds of labour, which affects a child's physical, mental, educational or social development.[1]

V. **Child trafficking** - child trafficking is the transportation, transfer, children for the purpose of exploitation. It is a violation of their rights, their well being and denies them the chance to succeed in their full potential. Child trafficking occurs when children are removed from safety and exploited.Children who are trafficked are frequently forced to work, used for prostitution, or just sold. Trafficking is any a part of the method from finding and recruiting children, to transporting and receiving them. Men, women and youngsters everywhere the planet isa victim of trafficking, but children are particularly in danger. Children who are trafficked are exposed to several dangers like working in hazardous environments. Many are also denied the chance to reach their full potential because they don't get an education or have the freedom to make their own choices.[2]

VI. **Bullying** - Bullying is essentially a sort of intimidation or domination toward someone who is perceived as being weaker. It is how of getting what one wants through some kind of coercion or force. It is also how for somebody to determine some kind of perceived superiority over another person. There are different types of bullying. While some might imagine that bullying mainly consists only of physical domination, the very fact of the matter is that there are verbal and emotional sorts of bullying also. And, with the rise of the Internet, there are now instances of children being bullied online through email, chat rooms and on Facebook. It is even possible to be bullied through text messaging on a telephone.Bullying can take any of these forms when it comes to children. For the foremost part, boys like better to use physical intimidation tactics in their bullying. They will use physical aggression to force others to try to what they need, or to feel responsible of a situation.Girls, on the other hand, are more prone to engage in subtle forms of child bullying, such as verbal abuse. Girls also are more likely to be adept at emotional bullying by ostracizing their victims or finding another thanks to make harass or belittle others.Bullying of children is a serious problem in schools around the country, and it is often highly destructive to children in the long run. Child bullying teaches them to require a particular view of what's normal in relationships with people and it also can damage their own self-image in ways in which can affect them for life.Bullied children are generally emotionally and socially stunted, and their academic performance suffers as a result. In some cases, serious depression and attempted suicide may result from childhood bullying.[3]

[1] Child Exploitation And Abuse, available at: https://www.savethechildren.org.nz/what-we-do/the-issues/child-protection (last visited on October 19, 2020).

[2] Chid Trafficking, available at: https://www.nspcc.org.uk/what-is-child-abuse/types-of-abuse/child-trafficking (last visited on October 19, 2020).

[3] Bulling and cyber bulling, available at: https://www.nspcc.org.uk/what-is-child-abuse/types-of-abuse/bullying-and-cyberbullying (last visited on October 19, 2020).

CHAPTER FOUR

Impact of violence

I. **Result in death**–There are some cases in which the victim beaten up the suspect to death.
II. **Severe injury** – the victims torture them. Risk of sexual assault.
III. **Mental health disorder** - Anxiety, depression, anger stress, trauma grooming, revictimization.
IV. **Unintended pregnancy** - Pregnancies that are unintended at the moment of conception are known as unintended pregnancies. Sexual activity without the use of effective contraception (pills, condoms) is the leading cause of unwanted pregnancy, whether by choice or compulsion.
V. **Communicable disease** - A disease spread by physical contact with an infected person, such as staphylococcus, sexual intercourse (gonorrhoea, HIV), fecal/oral transmission (hepatitis A), or droplets (influenza, tuberculosis), and dysfunctional sexual behaviour.
VI. **Emotional disorders** - emotional disorder occurs when an individual has difficulty regulating their emotions and it becomes a problem that is a danger to themselves or other people. These kinds of illnesses are both common and dangerous.

According to Indian study, between 18 and 50 percent of the country's population has been subjected to some form of sexual abuse at some point in their lives. Many children face to disclose the childhood abuse. In the state of Tripura, 160 boys and 160 girls from standard 8th and 9th grades were randomly selected. On average, 18% of the children had suffered sexual assault in the household.Girls had more incidents than boys. According to the data in India supported lengthy interviews with adults approximately 30% of men and 40% of girls remember having being sexually molested in childhood it was observed that 50% of abuse was done by family members and the other half with perpetrators.After a long period of time, the occurrence was also remembered in detail.[1]

According to the national crime records bureau (NCRB) statistics for the year 2018(the latest available), a total of6, 480 rape cases under IPC and POCSO were registered in Madhya Pradesh Of them, as many as 3,877 (60%)were minors.[2]

Child abuse statistics suggest that over 1,500 children in the United States die each year as a result of abuse and neglect. Furthermore, 75% of fatal child abuse victims are under the age of three, and parents are responsible for 78 percent of fatally abused children.One out of every three girls and one out of every five boys will be sexually abused before the age of 18. In some manner, 90 percent of child sexual assault victims know the perpetrators. A family member abuses 68 percent of people.[3]

In 2012, 82.2 percent of offenders of maltreatment were found to be between the ages of 18 and 44, with 39.6 percent being between the ages of 25 and 34.In the United States, about four children die every day as a result of child abuse and neglect. Boys (48.5 percent) and girls (51.2 percent) are about equally likely to become victims. Every year, 2.9 million incidences of child abuse are recorded in the United States.[4]

Parents, caregivers, classmates, romantic partners, and strangers all commit violence, according to the WHO. Globally 1 billion children aged 2 to 17 years have experience of physical, sexual, and emotional abuse. This violence can be prevented and for this WHO gave 7 strategies for ending violence against child that is INSPIRE[5];

I – Implementation and enforcement of law

Its basically encourages to ban the violent punishment of children by parents, teachers and other adults, together laws criminalizing perpetrators of sexual abuse and exploitation of children

N – Norms and value change

It basically emphasizes on the importance of changing harmful societal norms, which may target gender, ability level, age and other indicators.

S – Safe environment

It has found a reduction in violence by addressing "hotspots." Making environments safer may halt the spread of violence in a community all-together.

P – Parental and caregiver support

It provides ways of doing so, including home visits, group activities in community settings, and other evidence-based programmes that target parentsand caregivers. To stop violence against children it's very muchessential to engage the parents and caregivers.

I – Income and economic strengthening

It mainly focuses on the family's financial status. Its says that if Violence can often be prevented if a family's financial status improves so it's essence is to strengthen families' economic standing, including cash transfers, group savings and loans programs.

R – response services provision

It mainly provides examples of effective counseling and therapeutic approaches, screening combined with interventions, and treatment programs for juvenile offenders in the criminal justice system.

E – Education and life skills

It basically provides recommendations for increasing enrollment in preschools, primary schools and secondary schools, and relays the importance of safe, enabling school environments. Their agenda is to make child aware about violence and sexual exploitation so that children are less likely to become victim to such abuses.

[1]Deb S, Walsh K. Impact of physical, psychological, and sexual violence on social adjustment of school children in India, Available at: http://spi.sagepub.com/content/early/2012/02/01/0143034311425225 (last visited on October 19, 2020).

[2] Crime in India 2018 Report, volume- 1, Available at: http://ncrb.gov.in (last visited on October 19, 2020).

[3]Vincent Iannelli, Child Abuse is more common than any think, Available at: https://www.verywellmind.com/child-abuse-cases (last visited on October 19, 2020).

[4]Child Abuse Prevention Month, Available at: https://www.centerfieldcity.org/stay-informed/2015/4 (last visited on October 19, 2020).

[5] INSPIRE: Seven strategies for Ending Violence Against Children, Available at: https://www.who.int/publications/i/item/inspire-seven-strategies-for-ending-violence-against-children (last visited on October 19, 2020).

CHAPTER FIVE

Laws made and Act passed for the Protection of Child in India

A. **The Protection of Children from Sexual Offences Act (POCSO), 2012 (INDIA),**[1]

It is one of the legislation aimed at reducing child sexual violence. Aggravated penetrative sexual assault occurs when a child under the age of 12 is sexually assaulted. This offence is penalised by a fine and a minimum sentence of ten years in jail, with the possibility of life imprisonment.

Hands-on and hands-off

The broad definition of sexual violence against children includes both hands-on and hands-off abuse. Hands-on abuse requires physical contact between the perpetrator and therefore the victim. Examples are rape, sexual abuse and therefore the production of kid pornography. Hands-off abuse involves not physical contact between the perpetrator and therefore the victim, examples being watching kiddie porn or exhibiting sexual acts to persons below sixteen years old (sexual corruption). It should be always kept in mind that hands-off abuse often does maintain and induce actual physical sexual violence.

Digital and physical world

Sexual violence against children may occur both within the digital and within the physical world. Child porn has a clear digital element when it's distributed through the web. However, the abuse required to make child sexual assault images takes place within the physical or analogue world.

(B) The Juvenile Justice (Care and Protection of Children) Act, 2015.[2]

It was enacted to provide for children's ultimate rehabilitation through various institutions established under the law, as well as to take a child-friendly approach to adjudication and settlement of circumstances affecting their best interests.

[1] The Protection of Children from Sexual Offences Act, 2012, Available at: https://wcd.nic.in (last visited on October 19, 2020).

[2] The Juvenile Justice (Care and Protection of Children) Act, 2015, Available at: http://cara.nic.in (last visited on October 19, 2020).

CHAPTER SIX

Concept of Juvenile Justice System

The concept of "Juvenile Justice" has become quite significant and popular within the fashionable welfare society, with emphasis upon the welfare approach and protection of mankind, refers to the idea that the "state" because the last word authority, as guardian and caretaker, has both the right and obligation to direct and protect those of its citizens who, thanks to some impediments, demonstrate a requirement for such direction and protection.[1]

(C) Certain Statutes for the Protection of Rights of the Child

Even though the special legislations deals with children issues, there are certain provisions that are concerned about children in various statutes. Which are as follows: Family law, Employment law, Code of Criminal Procedure, 1973, Code of Civil Procedure, 1908, The Indian Evidence Act, 1872, The Indian Penal Code, 1860, The Immoral Traffic (Prevention) Act. 1956, Cable Television Network (Regulation) Act 1995, Narcotic drugs and Psychotropic Substances Act 1988, The Hindu Marriage Act. 1995, The Trade Unions Act, 1926, The Indian Contract Act, 1872 The Indian Trust Act 1882, The Indian Partnership Act, 1932 etc.

- **Rights of the child in Criminal law**

In India, under Indian Penal code 1860, there are ample of offence listed against the youngsters. As like, consistent with the section 82 and section 83, the children's are exempted from committing any crime.[2] So once we come to the generality of the provisions of both section it clearly says that a toddler below 6 years cannot commit a criminal offense and albeit he's quite 6 years and fewer than 12 years aged, they also cannot commit crime because they're not ready to understand the character, and therefore, the consequences of the act and crime. Therefore, a child below 12 years can't be prosecuted for any crime. Section 315and 316 of IPC talks about protection of kid that's killed before taking birth or after taking birth. This section prevents people from creating any quite problem to the unborn child from making him alive or causing him to die after its birth intentionally.[3]

(D) International Conventions for rights of the child

- The United Nations Declaration on the Rights of the Child, adopted in 1924.
- The Declaration of the Rights of the Child was adopted in 1959.
- The United Nations Convention on the Rights of the Child was adopted in 1989.
- The Committee on the Rights of the Child of the United Nations.
- The Universal Declaration of Human Rights was adopted in 1948.
- In 1966, the International Covenant on Economic, Social, and Cultural Rights (ICESCR) was signed.
- The International Covenant on Civil and Political Rights (ICCPR) was signed in 1966. A child has the right to a name and nationality, as well as proper nutrition, housing, recreation, and medical care, according to the Declaration.

(E) Constitutional Background

The Constitution of India guarantees a protective measures for the rights of Children. These rights are alienable rights, which have been especially for them to act always as a protective umbrella for the children. It includes:

• Rights to free and compulsory education for all children to the 6-14 years of age (Article 21A).[4]

This law was brought by the Constitution (Eighty-sixth Amendments) Act, 2002 which inserted Article 21-A under the Constitution of India. Article 21-A came into effect on 1 April 2010 that obliged the central and state governments to implements this fundamental right because it is enshrined.

• Right to be shielded from any hazardous Employment (Article 24).[5]

In India it was estimated in 2001 that approximately 120,000 children were involved in a hazardous job. Our Indian Constitution, under Article

24, it is strictly prohibited that the child labour below the age of 14 years cannot work in any factory or mine or engaged in other kinds of hazardous employment.

• **Right to be protected from abuse and occupations or forced by the economic necessity that is unsuited to their age or strength (Article 39-E).[6]**

In India, poverty is most difficult problem it is on the peak which leads the people to force their children for work at any kind of places. With this in mind, the writers of the Constitution created a policy under Article 39-E, which authorizes governments to set laws to ensure that children of tender age are not abused and that they are not pushed to pursue occupations that are unsuitable for their age or strength due to economic need.

•**Right to be provided equal opportunities and facilities to develop in a healthy manner (Article 39- F).[7]**

In India, our constitution itself provides an opportunity and facilities for the development of the children in a healthy manner with the conditions of freedom and dignity under article 39-F.It also ensures that the childhood and the youth are protected from exploitation and against moral and material abandonment.

Apart from it, there are certain rights for children that's are equally applicable to man and women or adult who are citizen of India.

[1] The Juvenile Justice (Care and Protection of Children) Act, 2015.

[2]Indian Penal Code (Act 45 of 1860), s. 82, 83.

[3]Indian Penal Code (Act 45 of 1860), ss. 315, 316.

[4] The Constitution of India, 1950, art. 21A.

[5] The Constitution of India, 1950, art. 24.

[6] The Constitution of India, 1950, art. 39E.

[7] The Constitution of India, 1950, art. 39F.

CHAPTER SEVEN

Judicial Pronouncement

1. ***In Peoples' Union for Civil Liberties v. Union of India,*[1]** it had been held that “Apart from the necessity of the International Labour Organization Convention, we have Article 24 of the Constitution, which, despite the lack of appropriate legislation, must “Proprio vigour” and because construction is clearly and absolutely a hazardous occupation, it is clear that no child under the age of 14 can be allowed to work in construction”.
2. ***In Unnikrishnan J.P. & Others v. State of Andhra Pradesh,*[2]**When the fundamental right to life (Article 21) is read in connection with the directive principle on education, the Supreme Court holds that the right to basic education is implicit (Article 41). The Court held that the parameters of the proper must be understood in the context of the Directive Principles of State Policy, including Article 45, which states that the state must strive to provide free and compulsory education for all children under the age of 14 within ten years of the Constitution’s inception.
3. ***In People "s Union for Democratic Rights v. Union of India,*[3]**The Court ruled that Article 23 has a broad and unrestricted scope, striking down "human trafficking" and "beggar and other forms of forced labour" wherever they are found. Article 23 prohibits not only being a "beggar," but also all other forms of forced labour. This text condemns forced labour, in whatever form it may take, as a violation of human dignity and a violation of core human principles. As a result, strikes also violate Article 21. The court ruled the government and its agencies to have a solemn constitutional responsibility to ensure that private individuals or non-governmental organisations properly apply the various laws, not only by it but also by others.

4. ***In Labourers performing on Salal Hydro Project v. State of Jammu and Kashmir and Others,[4]***It was decided that it is the responsibility of both the federal and state governments to ensure that any contractor or subcontractor on any of the projects' factories employs no Child under the age of 14. If a contractor or subcontractor uses a minor labourer, immediate orders for their break should be given as soon as possible, and an outline report should be sent to the sanctioning authority".
5. ***In Bandhua Mukti Morcha v. Union of India and others,[5]***It was decided that it was not right for the involved governments to turn a blind eye to the inhumane exploitation that bound labourers face." It is therefore critical that whoever government is in power acknowledge the existence of bonded labour and make every effort to remove it. In doing so, it will not only fulfil a humanitarian commitment, but also fulfil a constitutional responsibility and improve the country's participatory democracy foundations".
6. ***In Sheela Barse v. Union of India,[6]***The court determined that the child is a state blessing, and that it is the state's job to focus behind the child's perspective in order to ensure the appropriate development of its personalities.
7. ***In Jayakumar Nat &Anr vs State Of NCT Of Delhi &Anr,*** "The Delhi High Court orders the Government of the National Capital Territory of Delhi to come up with a proper plan to deal with the difficulty of rehabilitating those rescued children by providing some modest financial assistance so that their parents or guardians do not force them to work as child labourers again to meet their basic needs and supplement their income for their basic survival".

[1] AIR 1997 SC 568.
[2] 1993 AIR 2178.
[3] (1983) 1 SCR 456.
[4] (1984) 3 SCC 538.
[5] (1997) 10 SCC 549.
[6] 1986 SCALE (2) 230.

CHAPTER EIGHT

Recommendations and Conclusion

i. **Recommendations**

i. **There must be National Surveillance for Child Abuse.**

A strong closed-circuit television should be established in order that it is often easy for collecting multiple data across India. Such a system would improve the getting's of data about maltreatment and it might also leave a far better understanding of the magnitude of the matter and identification of the population at high risk.

ii. **There must be a scheme gone by the concerned government to form awareness about the child's right and their ways of higher growth.**

In the countries like India, people are more concerned about their earnings instead of protecting their child. So it might be better if a awareness program will inherit force. Which will make people aware of the child's right and their ways of growth. It happens mostly within the country where the literacy rate is extremely low.

iii. **A strong punishment should be imposed on people that send their child to figure and even those people that give the work to the Child.**

In countries like India, people have made tendency to send their child on work and luxuriate in their life on the earnings of the child. There are ample of family where the child has become the bread and butter of the family.

So, there must be a robust punishment gone by the parliament to prevent this sort of activity. It's also necessary that the one that gives the work to the child should even be taken into custody and that they must be hardly punished.

iv. **There may be a need of promoting empowerment.**

In India, there's a requirement of promoting empowerment in order that it'll facilitate the empowerment and children's participation that will enhance or make a culture of listening the youngsters and their safeties. Children's are a replacement learner of the skills; they build self-esteem and also develop an understanding of collaboration and their rights. Sometime children also feel that their views should be heard and valued.

v. **Principles of Person-centred values must tend priority.**

It is nothing but a guideline that helps in receiving care or support as a private interest at the Centre of everything we do like child's right, their dignity, Independence and even respect also. Once we see Article 21 of Constitution of India we see that each person (Child) have right to life and their personal liberties so if the Constitution is itself more concerned about the child's right then how people can deduct that right from the children.

vi. **Debate and discussion on child abuse and child protection issue**

Awareness of general public about child rights should be made through mass media propagation. Debates and discussions on child abuse and child protection issues can involve children to enhance the knowledge in public.

CHAPTER NINE

Conclusion

Child abuse prevention has become one among the main priorities of oldsters lately. Many children go from domestic ill treatment or abuse outside the house. Child abuses are often in any form whether it's mental or sexual assault, the consequences of both are very worst. The primary thing are often done is recognize the signs if a child is being abused. It is often difficult and therefore sometimes as abuse might not always be physical and the child might not speak out. The behaviour of a child should be observed. Sometimes a child suffers in silence and finds it hard to talk to anyone. It's a widespread problem. An individual who was sexually abused as a minor is at great risk of abuse. Children have a right to protection from sexual violence. The responsibility to supply children that protection lies with the authorities. The goal is to form people realize the pain child suffer in silence. In countries like India where poverty rate is so high that results in the oldsters to become more concerned about their earnings instead of concerning about their children's. So, its time to form people more aware of their children's welfare instead of concerning and giving more priorities to their earnings.

9 798886 298765

Printed by Libri Plureos GmbH in Hamburg,
Germany